# INCARNATE GRACE

Crab Orchard Series in Poetry
*Editor's Selection*

# INCARNATE GRACE

POEMS BY

## MOIRA LINEHAN

*Crab Orchard Review &*
Southern Illinois University Press
Carbondale

18  17  16  15    4  3  2  1

The Crab Orchard Series in Poetry is a joint publishing venture of Southern
Illinois University Press and *Crab Orchard Review*. This series has been made
possible by the generous support of the Office of the President of Southern
Illinois University and the Office of the Vice Chancellor for Academic Affairs
and Provost at Southern Illinois University Carbondale.

***Editor of the Crab Orchard Series in Poetry: Jon Tribble***

*Cover illustration*: Map detail from U.S. Geological Survey and Massachusetts
Topographical Survey Commission, "31. Boston sheet" (Boston: Topographical
Survey Commission, 1890); courtesy of the David Rumsey Historical Map
Collection.

Library of Congress Cataloging-in-Publication Data
Linehan, Moira, [date]
[Poems. Selections]
Incarnate Grace : poems / by Moira Linehan.
    pages cm.—(Crab Orchard Series in Poetry)
    ISBN 978-0-8093-3389-9 (paperback)
    ISBN 0-8093-3389-9 (paperback)
    ISBN 978-0-8093-3390-5 (ebook)
I. Title.
PS3612.I538A6 2015
811'.6—dc23                                              2014033227

Printed on recycled paper. ♻

The paper used in this publication meets the minimum requirements of American
National Standard for Information Sciences—Permanence of Paper for Printed
Library Materials, ANSI Z39.48-1992. ∞

*In memory of my parents—*
*Odette Wacha Linehan*
*and*
*Henry Linehan—*
*artists and my first teachers on how to look at this world*

# CONTENTS

# ACKNOWLEDGMENTS

My thanks to the editors of the following journals where these poems first appeared, sometimes in an earlier version:

*America*: "Last Wishes," winner of the 2010 Foley Award in Poetry, and "The Monks Who Made *The Book of Kells*"

*Crab Orchard Review*: "At Sainte-Chapelle" and "Wild Swans at Winter Pond"

*The Greensboro Review*: "Forty Years Ago"

*Image*: "For the Men Who Fish along Horn Pond," "Japanese Wall Hanging," and "The Sea Here, Teaching Me,"

*New Orleans Review*: "On Notice"

*Notre Dame Review*: "Praise Him in the Temple of the Present"

*Orion*: "That Moment"

*Poet Lore*: "Approaching 60" and "[the way you used to enter]"

*Poetry East*: "Against the Slow-Falling Snow," "For the One Who Still Lives inside Me—," and "Our Nature"

*Prairie Schooner*: "Brushes," "Vocation," "Waiting Room," and "*Woman Ironing*"

*Quiddity*: "Ferry" and "Naming It"

*Salamander*: "Balling Yarn" and "The Space Between"

*Sou'wester*: "My Great Blue"

*Tidal Basin Review*: "Scraping the Blackened Bottom"

*Weber Studies*: "In the Keep of the Body" and "The Plumber Said"

My thanks, too, to the editor of Outrider Press for including "Learning to Travel" in its anthology *The Mountain* (2014).

I thank the following for the time and space they gave me to work on many of these poems:

> The Virginia Center for the Creative Arts
> The Helen Riaboff Whiteley Center
> The Tyrone Guthrie Centre at Annaghmakerrig
> The Cill Rialaig Project

I also thank the research librarians at the Boston Athenæum and the Winchester (Massachusetts) Public Library for their patient and diligent responses to my many queries.

I remain grateful for the critical insights and support I received from those who read many of these poems in their various stages of development: Barbara Siegel Carlson, the late Sarah Getty, Marian Parry, Dawn Paul, Mary Pinard, Martha Silano and Myrna Stone. I am more grateful for the friendships that have developed from these connections. I am also blessed with so many family members and friends who believe in me and in my work. Their presence in my life is such grace.

Jon Tribble continues to have my abiding appreciation. Once again my work has been the beneficiary of his attention to every single line. But it is his vision for these poems as a collection that has been his greatest gift. I thank Allison Joseph for her incarnate grace. I extend my gratitude to members of the Southern Illinois University Press: Bridget Brown, Linda Buhman, Amy Etcheson, Wayne Larsen, Karl Kageff, and Austin Kodra. And once again, I appreciate Barb Martin's oversight of my poems.

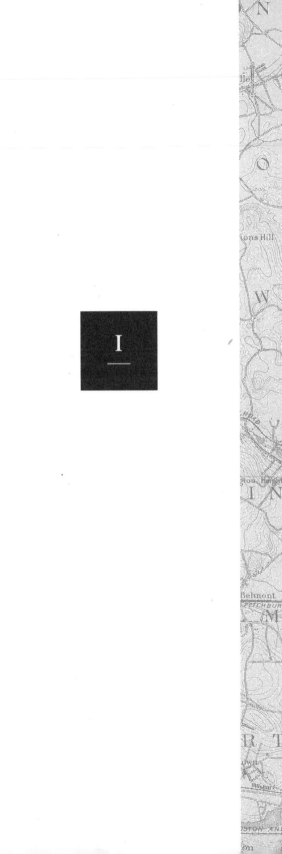

I

though who ever can? The present always
unwinding, slipping away—now in yarn
hand-spun and coarse, slips of thatch in the skein;
in seed stitch, in slip stitch, cable needle in front,
in back; in the back taking shape in ribbing,
in body and armholes, already stitches
for the neck band slipped onto holders.
Soon the warmth in my lap won't be enough
this dying afternoon, this season, this hour
for which the pond outside my window was named
Winter Pond, yellow-gray glow lowering
through the sky, now beneath clouds, now treetops
fanned out against the last light, this slippage,
this darkening, this now, already fled.

> *You can't collaborate or co-operate, except by sitting still*
> *and looking beautiful, in your own portrait.*
>
> —Henry James, to one of
> John Singer Sargent's sitters

I am my right breast pulled away from my chest,
spread flat against a cold glass plate, then pressed
flatter as the plate on top is lowered.
*Okay, don't move. Hold your breath.* I assume
she sees the lump I found, wants to see it
from another angle as she rotates the plates,
has me hug the machine with my left arm,
though she does ask if she may feel what I felt.
I am a right breast, a palpable lump
low at 8:00. *Don't move. Hold your breath.*
Between me and what I felt on my own
right breast, a glass plate remains. I can't get close
to what I feel. As soon as she's done, I'm ushered
into a very dark room. An ultrasound's next.
Gel over that breast, gel under that arm.
Then a wand bearing down, bearing down
as if to dig in. Her machine clicks away,
each click—a snapshot. At one point she rests
a ruler under the lump. Another click.
I have no say in the picture that's emerging.
Next day I'm back for a needle biopsy.
This doctor, a man. Suddenly, it's important
I am not my right breast. Only that breast
exposed. More than that breast exposed. *Hold still*
*for a pinch, a burning as I numb the area.*
He takes three samples, though I only hear
each extraction's startling gunshot crack.
He takes a fourth, then shows me the metal clip

he's going to insert to mark the lump. The lump,
I learn, did not show on the mammogram
I had yesterday. Had six months ago. *Not
uncommon*, he says. He has me have another
to make sure the marker's in place. Day one. Two. Three.
Day four. Day five. The diagnosis: invasive
lobular breast cancer. The kind that likes to hide.
That likes to move on to the other breast.
My next move: to an MRI of both breasts.
My cancer can't hide now. Forty minutes
I'll be in a tube on my stomach, arms
over my head, breasts hanging into a trough.
Inside the tube metal balls crash against metal walls.
I can't hear the music in my headset.
Forty minutes. *Don't move. Don't move. Don't
move.* What picture's emerging? Wanting both
breasts to be part of it, I don't breathe.

## WINTER POND

Three weeks ago, winter's first ice, not a skate blade
yet across its face. The town showed up: pick-up hockey,
the players' boots in piles for the nets; little ones
off to the sides, pushing old chairs, learning to stay up
on ice; babies in blankets, pulled around on sleds.
Who'd be thinking of the invasive plants massed below?
Days later it snowed. Left behind: an eight-inch cover,
powdery, light. In no time at all hockey rinks
were shoveled, the snow-mounds like rings of rolling hills
that froze in place. A week later, more snow. More
than a foot, but still powdery. Fierce wind gusts
churned the old mounds below to craters, left edges
with peaks. The dawn after that storm—Winter Pond,
a moonscape. The crater wall nearest me, mirror
of the blown-up image I'd been shown of the tumor
low in my right breast. Tumor to be cut out. Out
now. For the life of me, I can't picture a scalpel
skating along just under my breast, just above
my chest wall, each edge—the thinnest of margins.

*after* Winter *by Auguste Rodin, ca. 1890*

Even in this famous Parisian cemetery,
lichen-eaten slabs of the forgotten.

Early October, no sun for days. Grave tenders,
each working alone, sweep leaves from the paths.

Each time I walk here, I pass the same woman—
hair dyed the blackest, most unnatural black.
She carries her own small broom and watering can.
We have yet to acknowledge each other. *grave yard*

The anonymous and the tended, side by side.
Those with their ancient stones cracked, or missing,
next to those with their photographs encased
or sculptured as they were: here a young woman
in heels, long strand of pearls, seated with a book.

For Gertrude Stein's tomb: just her bold name
on an upright stone, white pebbles left one
by one on top. On the back, Alice's name.
Even in death she remains effaced.

Beyond the cemetery's open gate
Winter waits, her breasts hanging flat.

# NAMING IT

This gift. Like binoculars, so I can see
up close with both eyes what's out there. The weight
of it. I rest my elbows on my desk
to get a steadier look at this moment
at what is

        swimming toward me across the pond:
        lone brown duck, much smaller than a mallard.

What I see that I could not see without
this gift:
        white ring at the end of its bill.

Isn't this how I always want to look:
in the moment the distant brought in close
so I can read it in detailed relief?
I'm holding on with both hands so I can
take in what's here now in front of me:
        ring-necked duck migrating who knows where.

What I could not name save for these binoculars,
this new way of looking. This breast cancer.

## BALLING YARN

It won't stay balled, this slick rayon. Thick thread,
I'd call it, rather than fine yarn, the gray
and green variegated viscose I wind. Grays
of battleships and guns, fog, overcast skies,
then the greens: aquamarine and celery.
Skein, 320 yards, but now thickening
snarl. I have to follow the twisting line
twisted through tinsel, gray birch and pewter.
Those grays predominate, but among fish scales
and paving stones: occasional glimpses
of Caribbean waters and peacocks.
One slippery yard at a time I wind
a ball that won't stay wound, this ball I've balled
and reballed, finally think to secure it
with a rubber band I wrap around twice.
This will take days. I confess to cutting
the thread (more than once, mind you). I know.
I'll have dozens of ends to weave in
in the end. But for now I'm just relieved
to be straightening my mess, use a double-
pointed needle to pull the strand through and out
from the tangle. Again. Again. The lengthening
unruly yarn I want for an airy shawl
falls in long loops to the floor—loops that knot,
I stop to shake loose, unknot, start wrapping
around the growing ball I secure, yes,
with another elastic. I have three
more skeins, much heavier weights, to ball, same
metallic silver, aluminum, gray fox,
rain, a few settings of turquoise and emeralds.
The yarns' varying weights will give my wrap
the varied textures I want. An hour a day
I allow for this madness. Seven days

before I cast on 270 stitches,
cast off into the timeless knit-purl-knit sea.
On the horizon: breaching whales, skyscrapers,
flash of metal filings, fillings, hubcaps.
Shiny green mallard heads. Under approaching
storm clouds, gray-green backs of overturned leaves.

*In heaven, it was thought, only male bodies*
*would be resurrected.*
            —Eve LaPlante, *Salem Witch Judge:*
            *The Life and Repentance of Samuel Sewall*

Stomping upstairs downstairs all day yesterday
thinking Puritans men and women believed
banging pots I put away pounding out
two miles uphill on the treadmill only male
bodies pounding chicken breasts lopping off
the ends of green beans only male would be
resurrected in heaven women allowed
it was true lugging the glass storm door up
from the basement shaking out towels and sheets
from the washer the dryer this body mine
were I alive then but isn't that what Anne
Bradstreet meant what she knew *If ever two*
*were one, then surely we* Dan you and I
only yesterday scraping the blackened bottom
of one more pot without you each day a long
glass year it all lifts toward you oh won't I
*That when we live no more we may live ever.*

## IN THE KEEP OF THE BODY

Those preparing the body for the journey—
the one that begins in water, a barque
bringing it to the west bank of the Nile,
there to begin the journey that follows
the setting sun, its 12-hour pursuit of night—
first work a hook into the passageway
of the nose to draw down the brain (no use,

they believe, in this life, so none imaginable
hereafter). Next, the body turned on its side,
they cut an opening, reach in and take out
the organs. These the body will need again,
so these they preserve in canopic jars.
Each organ they remove except the heart.
The heart they leave in the keep of the body.

*

They leave the heart in the keep of the body
which they dry with salt. Seventy days it takes
to dry. Seventy days those left behind wait
before they fill it with spices, wrap it
in linen—the body with its companion
canopic jars, at last ready to embark.

Grief, meanwhile, has lost no time going to work
on the lover left behind, draining her,
then ferrying her to a desiccated place.
In dreams, already she is Isis, each night
finding her husband, one dismembered piece
at a time. Each piece she finds she reburies.
Each night she fails to find all of him.

## ELECTRIC

Fine line of my breast cells flush
On the brink between breast and
Right here—hard rope of a scar.

Tumor cut from that border—
Host breast/chest wall. Cancer had
Embroidered the milk glands there.

Left with a swollen right breast
I don't know—so erect, taut.
Fold line now scar line which tugs
Each time I reach with that arm.

On-going, electric—this
Fear as I lie in the dark:

*Margins clean but not ideal.*
Echoes of my surgeon's voice.

acrostic

# HEALING

When your breasts are already small. When your right breast is already
smaller than your left. When you find a lump in your smaller breast—
1.8 × 1.2 × 1.2 centimeters
the pathology report will say. When you add the margin
around the tumor, surely what was excised there in total—
no pound of flesh. Yet when you've already despaired of ever
attracting another lover. When you now examine day
and night your violated, scarred breast. When you see its swelling
diminishing, see that breast flattening some. When out of nowhere
thrusts of thin knives inside that breast mean nerve ends regenerating.
When that means healing. When you wonder when it will start for you.

> *Each mortal thing does one thing and the same:*
> *Deals out that being indoors each one dwells;*
> —Gerard Manley Hopkins,
> "As Kingfishers Catch Fire"

My late years. I want more
than ever to pray. Not
just sinking to my knees,
those lists of name upon
name on my lips day and
night. *Lord, let me add _____.*
Then his story, hers, takes
over. My voice grows shrill.
Of course that's praying. But
I long for the kind where
I sit before my pond
in the presence of what
*indoors each one dwells.* How
all artists remain in
what's made. The singular
hawk or the osprey. Each
picks as pew the same branch
in the elm, branching out
over the pond. It sits
hunched over. Other birds
congregate and chatter.
The red-tailed, the osprey,
sits and waits. Alone. Now
and then it turns its head.
Somewhere out there is food.

## AGAINST THE SLOW-FALLING SNOW

March 5th. The elm barren even of buds,
so it should have been easy to see the bird
landed amidst the scarred limbs. Its wing span
was what had caught my eye, the width of it—

no the swoop—its underside, mottled white
against the slow-falling snow. In the way,

too many branches. I had to get down
on the floor to look up under. If I can
just get this part right, the rest should follow.
Staring back through my binoculars: a face

streaked with black lines, deadly eyes, hooked beak.
Then it was gone. No time to make out more

except for a flash of pale red—as in the wash, red
bled on whites, *that* red in the opened fan
of its tail. Starved by the year's unending snow,
how I feasted on that ruin of color.

MARGINAL

What book, what exhibit, I can't remember where, the year
I saw those photos of women with mastectomies,
a fund-raiser, maybe a survivors' celebration,
was I alone, raw-red slashes, thin puckered sashes drawn down
one side of their chests, a branding, a lightning strike, what I knew
I'd never forget, maybe it was a documentary,
all those faces I see now, how soon afterwards were they
taken, there must have been dates, the whole world can damn well
go ahead and stare, those women of all ages, all sizes
of fierce, defiant remaining breast, how could I ever
join a support group about bras and prostheses, wigs—
lumpectomy scar, knotted crescent moon, cupping one breast?

## THE PLUMBER SAID

I'd have to live with it
until spring, the basement pipe running
to an outside faucet—frozen. So far
this, the coldest January since Cleveland
was president. I've been shutting that pipe off
and opening its faucet each fall for years.
*Don't you see how it slopes down toward this valve?*
What I'd noticed when I went to walk down
my driveway was a free-standing column
of ice just below the spigot, the plumber
saying I should also have been draining
that pipe inside, showing me how for next fall,
nothing else (he said) he could, I could do
until spring.

But when have I ever lived *with*
anything?—I who love things open or closed.
I who know foreboding each time I walk down
stairs, down cellar, now my driveway. You'd think
a widow had nothing more to lose. Frozen
pipes burst, that's all I've ever heard. Water
off, spigot open, mine (he'd said twice) would not.
Eventually everything thaws, even grief
so the second time around, attachment
clamps on ever more fiercely, the whole world—
or, at least, now my house—back for the taking.
I tell you, never have I been so long so cold.

last night just before it froze. That final
moment when the pond was still open water,

a fierce wind must have let go one long rush
the breadth of this pond, as if there'd been time

for it to go under, churn the water,

but not surface. Wind just as it was
coming back up, gasping through water turning

fixed. That moment caught now on the pond—
thick brushstrokes of gray curls, little trapped mouths.

## HALFWAY THROUGH RADIATION

*I went to the woods because I wished to live deliberately, . . .*
           —Henry David Thoreau, *Walden*

That stop-start again train that brought me to this point,
the endless local stops: finding the lump, doctor
visit, mammogram, ultrasound, needle
biopsy, repeat mammogram. The news. Surgeon
visit, MRI, preop tests, all the phone calls
in between before the lump, four lymph nodes—excised.
Then, back on the train: CT scan, bone scan,
oncologist, radiologist, onco-type
DX test results, radiation mapping, tattoos,
my vow the first time I lay on this table, johnny
half off, right arm above my head, three technicians
calling out numbers, red laser beams intersecting
on my exposed breast. In those crosshairs of intent
that first time, my vow (old, familiar): from now
on I will live this deliberately. Halfway through
radiation, though, day seventeen on this table,
it's already routine: 3:40 stop each afternoon,
beams set by the numbers. Mr. Thoreau,
tell me, what does it take to keep such a vow?

*In the end*
*It will not matter*
*That I was a woman. I'm sure of it.*
*The body is a source. Nothing more.*
         —Eavan Boland, "Anna Liffey"


My body's a lozenge in the world's mouth.
Not nothing. At least infinity's last
nesting doll. Maybe a nanosecond
of rain in the desert. Yet, in the end

even if my body's a pond, its name
*Winter* and the resident geese long gone . . .
even if it's a gargle of ocean swollen
by the earth's warming . . .
                it will not matter.

I'm sure of it: that I was a woman—
no matter how briefly, always in the face
of age and its diminishments—a woman
being called. The body is a source.

              Nothing more.
This body, here for the inevitable
disappearing and in so doing, soothing
a throat left raw by the unspeakable.

## WILD SWANS AT WINTER POND

Mid-September, my twenty-eighth autumn on Winter Pond.
Two swans with the year's two cygnets, heads immersed in the pond,

are feeding off plants below the surface. Years now the same
pair of mute swans has come back to breed on this small pond.

I'm sure they're the same two since each spring she chooses the same
spit of land for her nest. They have no purpose on this pond

save their own incarnate grace. And why don't I see my claim
as no less? No cygnet from her nest has returned to this pond

to breed. Only that first pair breeds here. I long to put a name
to what two returning swans have done for me. Winter Pond

and its history. All these years—to still have as your fame
an arresting glide of grace across the world. Winter Pond

and its mysteries. In May there were three cygnets. What's to blame
for one missing? I cannot stay forever on this pond.

I watch them paddle. Who will be the first to leave? I remain
transfixed. A pair of swans and their young contain me and a pond.

II

the way you used to enter
your childhood's dark stone chapel
small enough when you opened
the heavy door a deep in-
take of air excited rows
of little candles up front
by the altar rail a dime
maybe just a nickel you
slipped into the slot to pray
what could you have prayed for at
six or seven you wanted
your own flame your mother was
cleaning holy water fonts
back by the entrance baster
in hand to suck in the holy
water leave all the dust dirt
at the bottom of the bowl
your mother let you wipe it
clean just you and your mother
whispering *Yes just like that*
to walk back out into sun-
light hurt your eyes
                            all your life
you've carried some of that dark
safety your chapel bulldozed
to the ground a year or so
later a real church rising
near the spot it was never
the same empty chapel
an undisturbed hush exhale
that was you alone in what
in the silence the darkness
it really doesn't matter

where it's always before you
*shhh* stand again in that aisle
your mother's still behind you
walk pew by wooden pew keep
walking toward whatever waits
beyond railing locked gold door
on the altar emptiness
right side left just keep walking
something's always being bull-
dozed something's always rising

In times of need, I raise my eyes toward mountains
far west and north of where I live. Years it took
of return trips there before I imprinted them
within, made them a source. Now, the first days
of the long journey back from radiation,
the Blue Ridge spread out before me. The closest:
deep purple mountains bleaching toward the blues
of irises in those stacked behind; the farthest,
tinged far paler. Where they end and the clouds—
freighted with leftover snow—begin, I can't say.
But blest, I'd say, would be this woman,
this woman learning to travel, I'd say,
if she beheld mountains she'd never seen
and did not flee to those she carried within.

## THE PACIFIC MADRONE

Three madrones hang over the grassy edge
above the margin at Friday Harbor,
their peeling red-orange bark back-lit
by the rising sun. For years this stand of three,
twisting and bending around each other,
their bark swirling to follow the turnings,
the circuitous climbing of their limbs
endlessly after the light. The darkness above—
canopy of broad green leaves—their own doing.
How smooth the orange wood and beneath that,
the green exposed by the continuous
shedding. How public everything they are
losing, have lost, as the morning light burns
those ruddy thin strips of bark to sepia.

Let me have you come upon these birds as I did,
you, too, startling them into a sudden whoosh
as they rush under the brush along the same

wooded path I'll have you walk. You'll also have
something else on your mind, they'll vanish so quickly
you won't really see them though their scurry,

the gray-brown blur of their bodies, will register.
The next day ten or twelve will be running up ahead
along the edge of the sloping trail. Your footsteps

will send them for cover under the tall grass. This time,
though, you'll notice the dark plume jutting forward
from their foreheads. *Apostrophe*, you'll think. Now

you can turn to your *Sibley Guide* to find their name:
*California quail*, common to the West Coast
and so, here at Friday Harbor. Two days later

you'll get lucky. Outside the window by your desk,
a covey (your guide's word) as you look up:
a male atop a wooden chair, ten females

and the year's juveniles below on the path,
scratching, kicking up the dirt, pecking at the grass,
those motions as hurried as their running. The male

will remain stationary. You'll get to study
the overlapping blue-gray feathers on his chest,
the white outline around his dark face, that black

possessive plume each wears with such elegance, plume
composed, says Sibley, of six feathers. Though they can
fly, they prefer to run for their lives if need be.

# BIRDING TRIP, EARLY FEBRUARY, SOUTHWEST BRITISH COLUMBIA

The field guide's got sporadic green dots for it—
gyrfalcon, rare but possible in these parts—
one sighted, according to our leader, last week
near a train trestle so all morning we've looked
for bridges as places to stop along these fields.
No snow this close to the bay, we're in a good place
to find Arctic birds in winter. Any falcon
is new to me—the peregrine, kestrel, merlin
I've been shown so far. A gyr would be just one more.

Not so for the others on this trip. I'm out
of my element, these flats too vast to take in,
my field glasses not that high-powered. Three guys
have scopes so I've seen a falcon's hungry eye
up close. That's what I can't get out of my mind,
while in all the matte brown stubble someone, then
someone else, spots the gyr. I can't keep up
with the coordinates they're calling out—where
somewhere in the midst of this plain, there's a gyr

a quarter mile away. Even now they're stepping
back from their scopes. All I have to do is walk
over and I, too, can see it. I paid a lot
to come this far. Yet here I am once again:
up against a landscape so endless, I'm no more
than a singular green dot on the wide white
map of Canada, the hungry eye in my mind
I've never been able to satisfy, again
insisting, *No, no, no, this is not what I want.*

I who'd always lived a ways
away, at a distance, out
of sight, touch, days, weeks alone,
inside, behind, yes, without
connecting. Now, 180,
at the very least going
to, toward, approaching them, all
my beloved still on this
earth, I want them by, around,
near, close, next to, alongside,
with me, these days want the links,
the bindings, the fasteners,
the clips, the glue, tape, and string.
But back then, in those times,
earlier, back when, before,
wouldn't I have loved this law
regarding, on behalf of
orcas off, among, between
the San Juan Islands, that law
silk-screened in blues on posters,
the backs of T-shirts, *Get off*
*my tail*, hundred-yard order
to boats to back off, stay back,
give those beauties right of way.

## FERRY

The day's last ferry, slipping out for the mainland,
each window on its many decks lit before me,
a Frank Lloyd Wright design, clean-lined stained glass,
upon the nighttime waters. Barely moving—
this ferry, its reflection—and I'm held on shore
at a window. In six days I'll walk back into
its hungry mouth. In sunlight's glare that ferry's mouth,
blacker than the woods tonight behind me.

Beyond the harbor, the ancient boatman's rowing,
rowing since the world began, coming toward me
in his open dinghy, ferryman for what will be
my passing. The island's ferry's passed. Or Charon's
already claimed me as his passenger, so slowly
do we glide I don't even know I'm on board.

Ahn:

> Anointed *Anon.* anew.
> Anathema here, too. For like
> Anubis, I guard many tombs.

Ahnne:

> Nettles in the roadside hedges:
> Necrologies. The margins where I walk.
> Netherworld, I'm coming, my head high.

Ahnnema:

> Mahler skyscape: full moon rising, tormented clouds. *Danse*
> *Macabre.* One year ago today, a malignant lump.
> Mama, it felt like a piece of a pencil in my breast.

AhnnemaCARE:

> Care for, can you (hear the stress here), land too boggy to farm?
> Care for, can you, drumlins, the refuse of glaciers?
> Care for, can you, this greenery? Without rain, no green.

AhnnemaCARErig:

> Rigging in place for my vessel to sail.
> Rig ready. Even my fishing line
> Rigged and baited. Today, only the cold biting.

Annaghmakerrig.

> *At the Tyrone Guthrie Centre*
> *at Annaghmakerrig, Co. Monaghan*

Before windows facing west-southwest
I knit during late autumn's long sunsets,
the lingering twilight here. At this point
in the scarf lengthening on my lap,
I don't need the pattern. I'd wanted one
that mirrored the letters I'd studied
all summer long, letters elongated as vines
and tails, then decorated with arabesques
along their curves. These reversible cables
twisting in columns, front and back, my yarn
dark blue heather. Raised texture I finger
row's end, row's start, checking for errors. I ripped
what I'd knit so many times in the beginning
till I got the tension I wanted, understood
what the chart did, and did not, show.
I belong to a long line of women
who made their own patterns, their own stitches.
Like those monks, their own script for the Scriptures
they copied. *Just keep track of what row you're on.*
What line. Yes, errors in the text in *The Book
of Kells.* Yet scholars proclaim that book
*perfect*, its wide margins clean, nowhere
a trace of marginalia. My surgeon's voice,
ever coming back to me: *margins clean
but not ideal* around the lump she'd cut out.
Again, that pause. As monks had their readers do
with the resting cats they inserted at the ends
of sentences, the ends of verses. Ever that pause.

Who were they?—the monks who made this book,
the scribes and artists, once fishermen and farmers,
this son or that a father had given as tithe,
the orphans—left as infants, as children—
who stayed the rest of their lives, and those few
suffused with a sense of a calling. Men
who wore goatskins over their tunics, sandals
in the extremes of heat and cold. *The Rule*
stressing obedience, order infused
throughout the day: when to pray, to work. Fast
on Wednesdays and Fridays. Conversation
kept to a minimum. Diet, as routine:
vegetables, peas, beans, a small loaf of bread.
Milk and butter. Beer. Those close to the sea,
seal meat and fish. Scholars able to say
four such men copied these gospels, Hand
A, B, C, D, they call them, making the part
suffice for the whole. Who were they? If *The Rule*
had to remind them to read what they wrote—
yes, errors in text passed down book to book—
what's the fission, what's the fusion that explains
such abundance amidst the austere:
two thousand initial letters enlarged
and colored, then embellished with flourishes
of tendrils and spirals, interlacing knots,
serpents undulating around and through,
not one design in this book repeated?

# THE ART OF MANUSCRIPT ILLUMINATION

Before they were monks, they were fishermen,
they were sailors, they knew the knotting of ropes,
how to tighten, how to loosen, eyes closed,
could interlock knots into nets, hands moving
over and under, around and back. Twisting
and turning, that rhythm flowing in and out
through their hands, illuminating the texts
they copied, margins set off with fretwork
and lacework, letters entwined with tendrils
and vines, grapes for the picking. *I am the Vine*,
they wrote, wrapping serpents around chalices.
*. . . So must the Son of Man be lifted up.*
Their homeland's art—roadside crosses and pendants,
sweaters and bowls—in metal, enamel,
stitchwork and stone. Spirals and cables, left
twist and right. Art they made, art they wore.
Down through the ages, art at their fingertips,
eyes closed, these monks who knew the knotting of ropes.

Monstrous margins of wild seas surround his island.
In the scriptorium, measured margins enclose
the wondrous words he's arranging on paper. Margins
as frontiers from whence come creatures—flying or running,
swimming or crawling into the lines, finding letters
to curl in, gnaw on, wrestle, pin to the page.
Illumination putting flesh on each word.
Christ as Word, once again made present by the hand
of a scribe, a monk with his quill moving letter
unto letter, old page of text copied onto
the new, despite the room's stone chill, despite the ache
along his neck's right side. Weeks before this part
of the story comes unto its end. On this page
the Word again the Way, offering passage
across the border to the Kingdom within.

CROSSING OVER


*This close to the border. So close. Just up*
*a ways. Just over that . . . How close depends,*
one says at last, *which road you take.* Roads
north, east, west of here at Annaghmakerrig
will take you there, the border using the land
and its contours, hillocks and rises, rivers
and streams to draw the line—this the Republic,
that Northern Ireland—all along the way,
the border twisting and turning, winding
back on itself, dipping down and around
where it just was. Finally one says, *Fifteen*
*minutes,* how close. Now I'm getting somewhere.
Here to Newbliss, on to Clones, then over
into the country I've heard about, read about
back in Boston forty years now, the North,
the Troubles, the hunger strikes and shootings,
the bombings and beatings. All the processions
behind coffins carried on men's shoulders
to churches, to gravesites. This, the boundary
I should not cross over, it is not safe,
I, a Catholic. The man who's offered
to take me wears an orange parka. Peace,
more than ten years now. *I want to walk over,*
I tell him and he stops the car this side
of a slight rise in the tarmac, no line,
no gate, no guards. *There never were any,*
he says, *this far out in the country.* Not even
a sign we're entering County Fermanagh,
only the change in speed limit signs: red
and black on white in the North, just black on cream
in the South. I cross over, cross back, stand
one foot in each country. He has me follow him
to look for the water that shapes the divide.

It's not even a stream. A trickle, at best.
*See there, coming around here and that hedge*
*over there is likely where it continues,*
*then on up that hill.* Back in the car, he drives
into the North though not for long. Sure enough
the water winds back and, slight dip in the tarmac,
we're back in the Republic. This, the way it goes.


*for Steve Hanson*

# CILL RIALAIG ELEMENTAL

*Ballinskelligs, Co. Kerry*

Ah, it's the sky does it every time, bursts each of my seams,
Insinuates itself, billows me into a kite. Winds catch me,
Rip open my hidden pockets, expose layers of padding.

\*

Waves amassing today far out in the North
Atlantic, sucking in their fury. Then, suicidal,
They rage the length of the bay, plow into the cliffs.
Evidence scattered everywhere—spray, mist, fog, drizzle,
Rain. Always under their terror here.

\*

Elegiac this, the end of Ireland where rocks
Arrange to repeat themselves: outcrops, rock walls
Round fields, more walls dividing those fields. The enclosed.
The emptied. A few morose cows under stone skies.
High on the hills, more outcrops. Or slow, grazing sheep.

\*

First kindling, then peat, then again those layers, and a match.
In my head, so simple. But the wind works its way inside. I
Resign myself each twilight to the hour to start it. Inside this
Eremitic cottage, small duties to keep at bay night's dark.

Late day the bay's far hills, shades of desert-rose
though the bay itself has gone gray. All day, clouds
rowed in with the sea, not as banks or trains.
Rather, each was its own presence. On a day
more sun than shadow, even the darkest
did not seem to carry rain. In the darkening
blue air along the clouds' dark undersides,
the tallest mountains over there have begun
to blur. Drop by measured drop, fading light
stains the rest of the sky the bay's gray. Clouds
start to congregate, move as one. Their shadows,
trails of purple swaths. The last light shines on the last
mountain. Moments ago, this side of the bay
had been set in shadow. Now the few distant
white houses—along with their fields and containing
rock walls—glow in a warm wash. And as quickly
return to shadow. Across the bay a line of lights—
house lights? street?—flicks on. Car lights
move toward home. Twilight lingers, no hurry
to leave. For who is there to meet us?

## JOURNEY TO SKELLIG MICHAEL

Whatever their reasons for going there—
those fifth-century monks—mine for coming
to Ballinskelligs from where they left. From where
I've taken a boat to follow them out
into the North Atlantic, those monks who rowed
and rowed against this bay's pent-up sea, though
right now the sea, the calmest since I arrived.
Our boatman's skill, hitting each oncoming wave
dead on, this small boat's rise and fall through the bay
and round Bólus Head till we see in the distance
the rock where we're headed, jutting straight up.

But even the calmest sea should not
be taken lightly. I know by now not to
take any journey lightly, though I've come
with only a dream and waterproof clothes.
Maybe here at last I'll understand why
all my life I've sought places monks went:
monasteries, retreats, outlying ruins.
The isolated, far-flung. This jagged rock
falling from view and rising back up
as our boat descends into trough after trough.
A good hour or more. Are we getting closer?
The monks would stay seven centuries.

What draws me to places desolate
as this shard of rock, remnants of its monks'
small stone huts along terrifying ridges?
There's a small stone shelter in me. I've learned
that to go inside there, stay any length
of time, I need to be far away, so far
it's the only place left. For once inside,
refuge is found. Not of my own making.

Nor fixed in stone. But refuge, nonetheless,
that steadies me for what sometimes seems
like only an hour, sometimes seven centuries.

Not today, though. This early November day,
the wind that's come up has churned the sea,
made landing too risky. Waves, breaking over,
being sucked back from the small concrete slab
that passes for dock at this rock's base.
Waves, swinging our idling boat. The boatman
at long last begins the slow curve back
to Ballinskelligs. Even with the sea
coming from behind, it's too rough for me.
I can't look back. Shard of Skellig Michael,
now lodged inside me. How long was I there?

*Go outside and stand on the mountain*
*before the Lord; the Lord will be passing by.*

*A strong and heavy wind was rending the mountains*
*and crushing rocks before the Lord—*
  gales turning waves into canyons,
  into crevasses, their drop-offs
  sheer as the iron cliffs here
  at land's end. Today's storm, playing
  handball with what sounds like boulders
  smashed against those cliff walls.
  Hundreds of feet above
  in my cottage, I've never longed so
  for silence—
*but the Lord was not in the wind.*

*After the wind there was an earthquake—*
  the stove's glass door rattling, metal
  frame on metal side. I wedge a chair
  under its handle to keep it
  from shaking. I've locked myself in
  to jam the front door tight in its frame.
  Earlier the outer back door
  flew loose, drummed a tattoo
  against the cottage's stone siding.
  When I couldn't relatch it,
  I threaded the stove's thin poker
  through its loops and into the hole
  for its bolt. All I've done is bring
  the upheaval's roar inside—
*but the Lord was not in the earthquake.*

*After the earthquake there was fire—*
        those waves now like flames, like tongues
        climbing the sides of the cliffs, hungry
        to lick every inch of their slam-dance
        partners, wanting them on their backs,
        those insatiable waves pushed
        up and up—
*but the Lord was not in the fire.*

*After the fire there was a tiny whispering sound.*
*When he heard this,*
*Elijah hid his face in his cloak*
*and went and stood at the entrance of the cave.*
        Who could ever hear a whisper
        in this place? Elijah, how will I
        know when to follow you back
        to the wilderness we came from?

*1 Kings 19: 11–13*

the sea saying, *This is how you pray*
*to your rock of a god, your massive cliff*
*of a god, sheer drop into the bay,*
*immovable, not-going-anywhere*
*kind of god. Look at photos from a hundred*
*years ago. Your god's not moved. Glacial remains*
*of a god. Impenetrable. Can't-wear-it-*
*down god. Rock face of a god. Face it.*
*You're a dot on the landscape, a sheep's droppings*
*before this god.* The sea telling me, *Maybe*
*the wind will side with you. Maybe it won't.*
*So you wait, wait for a day in November,*
*a day like yesterday, the wind wild*
*off the Atlantic, but backing you up,*
*making you come wave upon wave face to face*
*with the wall of your god.* Telling me,
*You stand up as wave, are shattered to spray,*
*lifted as mist. You keep being lifted up*
*and over the fields beyond that cliff, mist*
*falling now over the matted wet wool*
*on the backs of sheep, their faces pushed*
*into grass.* The sea, teaching me to say,
"So be it. So be it."

III

BRUSHES

In China, the first were made for writers—
rabbit hair wrapped round with the hair
of deer and sheep. Ogishi demanded
feelers from around the rat's nose

and hairs from the kingfisher's beak.
The early handles were mulberry stems.
Soon, official documents could be written
only by scribes holding red lacquer handles.

By the time ivory was required,
writers kept them in gold jeweled boxes.
They say it took fifteen years to master
how to hold one. Even children at play

with their chopsticks, trying to pick up
just one grain of rice, were learning the art
of longing—that implement the only
ferry now to the other side of desire.

# JAPANESE WALL HANGING

The brush might absorb too much water.
Not enough. His stroke could be too heavy
or hesitant. The ink could blot. Refuse to
spread. Spread in the wrong direction.
The Japanese brush painter has trained
for years to face this moment. On his knees,
leaning back on his heels, today he pictures
the heron, come back season after season
to the small pond behind his house. Hours
he's waited there for the drift of its descent,
for that floating line to take over.

*after* Portrait of Anne Page *by Dennis Miller Bunker*

In the gallery a woman's lecturing
about the rose the artist placed on the table
next to his subject. A rose bloomed, the bloom

past now for the woman who should have sat
a few years earlier for her portrait.
Regret fills the space between them—

the woman on the canvas and the woman
who talks about what she's become. The onlookers
in front of the portrait begin to shift

one foot to the other, shifting the portrait
in and out of view for those behind them.
It should be no surprise the woman speaks

more about the rose than the woman she is
faced with. The rose—petals curling, each one
splayed and pressing down, each one a breath held:

as long as nothing moves. Regret could be a wish
nothing more move. At least, not for the woman
lecturing a group now anxious to move on.

It should be no surprise. The artist painted
only what he saw, though in the space
between, the future has appeared: all that is
no longer possible. All that hangs by a breath.

# PREDESTINATION

*Rijksmuseum, Amsterdam*

Rembrandt's placed Rebecca on Isaac's lap,
her dress of ruffled red brocade, billowing out,
gradually blurring into the background,
a shadowed garden. *The Jewish Bride*, her gaze
averted from the viewer and from Isaac,

though his right hand rests just below her breast,
though her left hand holds his there while her other
cups the gold-lit place on her lavish gown
where she's still a virgin. Rembrandt shows her
calm, ready. I would not say she's eager.

This, after all, is Calvinist Holland
where men in wide-brimmed hats—like the black one
Isaac wears—do not smile for a Rembrandt.
From the way his hand lays a quiet claim
on her body, I'd almost believe that *if*

Isaac goes through with this, he'll wait for her
to say *Yes* each step of the way. I say *if,*
though, because of his gaze—it, too, averted
and shaded, the whole left side of his face
removed from view. His gaze is what stopped me

in the first place, what's held me on this bench.
For much of our short marriage, my lover
was dying. That might be darkening my vision.
But as the hours before this wedding night
turned into days of posing, it seems one

of them—Rembrandt, the model—sensed Isaac
had had second thoughts. This now the moment
of the painting: Isaac remembering
his father's god has a plan for each
and every chosen one. There was for mine.

## VOCATION

Without the title, I'd never have guessed
*Self-portrait as the Apostle Paul.* The apostle part,
I mean, for by now I know Rembrandt's face.
Here at fifty-five, the artist masquerading
as that fiery man near the end of his life,
quieted, reading the Scriptures—a book
in this painting, as if the printing press
had always been around. Though had it been,
Paul could be rereading one of his own

epistles—*First Corinthians, Second.* Each time
he looks back, Rembrandt likewise finding
something he's left out or at least, one more way
to show what he means: *Self-portrait Frowning,*
*Self-portrait Leaning Forward, Self-portrait*
*as a Beggar, as a Burgher, Bareheaded,*
*in a Soft Hat, in a Plumed Hat,* even
as a saint. Yet I should not have said "reading
the Scriptures" as if to suggest Paul had been

pondering their words, trying to see
how much still holds true this close to the grave,
because Rembrandt's pictured Paul, or himself,
having just looked up, having just been called
from his praying, his painting. *Who wants what now?*
Interruption could be the summation
of this life. Even at fifty-five, still the need
to discern: *Temptation? Invitation?*
*What's the hunger I've been put here to feed?*

Here where someone believed the roof's weight
could actually be carried off and down
into arms of stone; where someone had faith
the structure would hold these glass windows rising
toward vaulted reaches; architect or glazier,
sure this light stained red and blue was fitting
reliquary to house the crown of thorns
Louis IX had purchased from the Emperor,
the saintly king never doubting it was
kept as relic some twelve hundred years.
The scam of that sale at war within me here
where a saint once prayed, I paid seven euros
to enter. I'm nothing more than a tourist
here for the moment, caught up in some streaming
red and blue air. It is enough, though, it is
more than enough, I believe, right here right now.

## FORTY YEARS AGO

on the shady side of this cathedral
in lace bonnets stiff and tall as baguettes,
selling doilies and pillowcases, placemats
and napkins, anything that could be trimmed

with lace, trimmed with lace; dolls like themselves,
long blue skirts, white aprons heavily starched:
on my mind but now nowhere, not shady,
not sunny side of the cathedral I circled,

not the surrounding narrow streets I wandered—
lace makers nowhere to be found. So back
I went, this time went in, blue of the stained glass,
blue of those skirts—memory appliquéd

on the moment, stitch work so fine, women
went blind. Later, looking back from the station
at the towering north side, the missing still
on my mind, there in stone relief—homage

to the work those masons watched their mothers,
watched their sisters and aunts, even rows of nuns,
turn out. The finest silk thread for the edge
of a sleeve. The wheel of that Rose Window.

## WAITING ROOM

They must have been adding up—all the addling
portrait stares, Samurai swords, slashes of black
across stretched canvas. And the man I'm with

who won't leave a museum till he's read
every inscription. He's galleries behind
and we still have two levels to get through.

Yet as I come into this unfurnished room—
Chapter House from a Benedictine priory
not far from Saint-Germain-du-Bois—all that eases.

Here, the one place where those medieval monks
could speak—who was to do what for the week,
the year. Their lives like the limestone bricks

wedged into this vaulted Romanesque ceiling—
numbered, dismantled, transported, then reassembled
inside a new space in this city where Elizabeth

Bishop once waited for her Aunt Consuelo.
An enclosure, still ordering the lives
of anyone who enters. This empty room
where the I that I am is now coming back.

*WOMAN IRONING*

Back, at last, where I belong: on this bench.
Back in front of Degas's *Woman Ironing*,
my washer woman steadfastly at work,

leaning close over a man's white dress shirt,
already the balm of her composure
beginning to soothe. Her flat iron steams

in the steamy room where bed linens hang—
ceiling to floor—before a wall of windows,
sheets still clinging to dreams and sheer curtains

billowing in the warm, cream-colored light.
A plump woman in a dark blue blouse,
ample rose apron—each press of her iron,

rhythmic and composing. How many blues
have been shaded throughout the man's shirts,
one set off to the side of her work table,

pressed and folded, those folds exact, and exact
the starch in its high collar. She reaches
for the next, though surely she must know

at the ballet this evening or the races
tomorrow afternoon, Monsieur's shirt
will barely make an impression, at best will
merely reappear as a smear of white paint.

*The National Gallery of Art*
*Washington, D.C.*

At row's end I turn the scarf, row just purled,
purling every even row, turn to work the lace

stitches for the holes, *knit two together, knit three,
yarn over*, over and over counting the stitches

in the odd row of rows numbered 1 through 24,
rows for the open panes. I take pains to count

44 stitches at each row's end, knitting the black wool
into raised lace diamonds, settings for small circles

of rosettes within, webbing of *yarn over, knit three
together, yarn over* to hold those rosettes in place.

Within the pattern of repeating 24 rows,
the relief when the next must be purled. I fly

through every purled row, while at its end the next
painstaking one waits for me to turn my scarf.

Isolated in late daylight they wait—
stone blocks along the pond's low-lit edge.
They were here yesterday. They will be here
tomorrow, seeking an animal all mouth
and mute. Something about these men drew Christ.
Was it their knowing there would be fish, and fish
appeared? Surely the faith He'd want from them
required expectation, that long wait
for the bite.

\*

*Ma, tell her she can't come. She talks*
*too much*—my brother's whine that time I said
I, too, was going fishing. But, though I was
older, my mother sided with my brother,
my mother who used to row her father's boat
and clean his fish along with those she'd caught.

\*

I'm older now and still have never fished.
And my faith? Well, these days it's too flat and bony
to hold much meat. Maybe what drew Christ
was that those men He would make preachers
could withstand silence. And not just their own—
that of those beside them, too. I can't
be so long so empty. Why a lifetime later
I might still be seeking that something
so awake its eyes are always open.

It's not in our nature to leap
like fish into the other world

above and shine. But haven't you
at least once followed the arc

of a lone fisherman's line,
the long cast taking you out

over the deep part of the pond
till you, too, hang suspended?

And for the one breath you are
held there, aren't you boundless,

even though the line's already
begun to shudder, fall to earth?

## ON NOTICE

Gradually approaching along twilight's long grade,
Right edge of the pond steeped in a tea-colored haze:
Elder statesman, taking all the time he wants
Arriving. Ancient turtles, settled in the algae-
Thick muck. Red fox, already trotted through. Descending,

Broom-like legs sweeping the evening air behind his back.
Long steady wing beats bringing him in, so that his cry—
Ungainly as his attempts to fly back to where-
Ever he comes from—sets my teeth on edge. That cry,

Hoarse and harsh. More squawk than measure of any song.
(Even so, his solitary bent holds his wings back.)
Rabbinical that cry, from a country no longer
On the map. Perhaps it never was. But now serving
Notice: on my pond this arriving, still coming in.

Eventually even my grief would leave me.
Late November: the great blue's lifting off

for the season, though maybe it doesn't
yet know that. Surely I don't. Who doesn't know more

afterwards? Those moments after the bird's decided
but before it's the thinnest of barques slipping through air,

those in-between moments—wings seeming to beat air
in vain—unbearable to watch. The body

and the endless rearrangements it undergoes
to rise again. There's no doubt I'd gone under.

Throughout my long season of grief, life came and went
on this pond. Wrong to say the heron decides.

The light shifts. So, too, the pressure on the hollow
bones of birds, widows. My great blue came and went.

FOR THE ONE WHO STILL LIVES INSIDE ME—


buzz, sting, maker of honey, who keeps
alive flower and fruit, butterfly
and bird. And inside me still, his twist,
his swivel to notice, to follow
the world's dazzle, its drama in red
heads, red flashing lights, Red Fez Café,
every spice known to man, blistering
heat—yes, all holding out a tango,
everything sultry with sweat. Inside
still, free fall of wings that open mid-
air, mid-stream, mid-sentence, floating me
back to those places no one gets to
alone. Remembering afterwards
the singing. The singing afterwards
in the wake of re-entry. Morning
after morning he remains. I remain.

striding forward, this the moment she—single winged—
is going to plant the ball of her left foot, same
moment she's lifting her right heel off the ground,
she's up on her toes, feet arched as if in high heels,
watery blue-gray statue walking, knees locked,
left knee, the two blocks from the scrapyard it came from
still attached, blocks mirroring her right hip's box-shape,
her thin legs two sides of a triangle, grounding
this woman, no arms, no head, but fixed winged
and approaching, her torso ravaged, gouged
top and bottom, sternum cracked, single wing raised
as shell, kite, shield above her rough right shoulder,
its bronze patina closer to gold, counter-
weight, she's over nine feet tall, she's rising.

*

No, come at her as shadow
against the gallery wall,
the angle of the lighting
arching her chest, thrusting it
up, her head (had she one) thrown
back. My body remembers
this ascending, taken out
of myself, oh yes, like this.

*after* Winged Woman Walking I
*by Stephen De Staebler*

## AFTER THE STORM

First thing I notice: two kestrels back, right outside
my window, hanging fixed in the air, chests out
against the wind's furor off the sea, tilting—
just slightly—wing to wing to stay in their hover
above the chasm between the two cliffs below.
Minutes tick by. The two of them teetering,
eyes searching side to side the grassy slope to rock,
rock to vicious foam. What did they do yesterday
in those gales, walls of rain driven in from the bay?
My small window, so pummeled at times I could not
see out. Today's winds, diminished but still pushing back
at whatever comes toward them. These small birds,
feathers the color of wet dark granite, suspended
on wafer-thin wings above a precipice
and a sea with no food for them.

When I go to leave this world, how do I
take with me the grace it held out, it held
onto, when I go, that momentary grace
I caught now and again as I'd look up,
look out? Once, late afternoon, a March wind
swaying the elm, the shadows Matisse's

blue cutouts, thighs thick as limbs dancing
over the rumpled snow on such delicate
pointed feet. Once, columns of snow swirling
across my pond and I saw stampeding
horses, saw again those sheep outside Dingle,
a dog driving them, left then right, lower

to upper field. When I go, that streaming once
more mine. Or when I go, the sudden rising
of hundreds of swallows banking as one,
then banking again. That nearly closed arc
of an Arctic tern's wing turning in flight.
When, when to the next wherever I'm going—

mound, mountain, lap of God—let my leaving
be its own imprint of grace: the eagle
I once saw drift down over a river,
extend its talons, graze the water, and lift.
The imprint of that long, slow swoop—what's first
and last remembered when I go. Then, only then,
the shock of it: prize fish taken out of its world.

## A DEEP WOUND

*Cill Rialaig, Ballinskelligs, Co. Kerry*

The one thing we're said to have in common,
those of us with breast cancer: a deep wound.
For one year I said *Yes* to that hard truth:
the forty-five years back to the morning
my mother did not wake up. I said *No*,
for too many women have this disease.

Now at Cill Rialaig, I see how land, too,
can hold a deep wound. Eight stone dark cottages—
set side by side and back from the cliffs—keen
in the footprints of what once sheltered
those who lived here; farmed that one crop

in this endlessly gray, rock-strewn land;
fished herring from the bay before them.
Cottages restored in memory of those
driven here by a great hunger. Driven
away by one greater. Or in memory

of those who starved here, died, and were buried.
Here, still a place more of the abandoned
than the restored. Along the one-lane road,
the remains of so many walls, some with outlines
of windows and doors. Layer of thin rock

on layer of thin rock. All of them missing
their roofs. Weeds, where once there'd been floors.
Even the herring no longer swim here.
Remnants of monks' rounded huts, running
on a sightline dead center through my cottage

down to priory ruins by the bay.
*Rialaig*, from Irish words for "followers"
or "regulars" and "of the rule," as in monastic
rule. *Cill Rialaig*: Church of the Regulars
where I'm now a follower. A sacred space

with a hundred-fifty-year-old wound. How long
does it take for a soul to leave this earth?
I left Boston on the Feast of All Saints,
arrived here the Feast of All Souls. Holy days,
their origins in the spirits of the Irish

dead and the truth that the veil between this
world and one beyond does open, if only
for an evening a year. Opens this time of year
when winds and any moon pull the sea to the edge.
Can pull anyone trying to sleep there,

even those who sleep the sleep of death.
Those who, without waking, are known to rise
at this time of year and walk the places
of their great hunger. So tonight, the sea wild
to summit the cliffs below, if those souls

should do just that, let them visit me on this
grieving gray rock. Let them bind up my deep wound.
Let them caress the scar beneath my right breast
that never stops aching. Let them, if just for this night.

# NOTES

The title of "Praise Him in the Temple of the Present" is a line from Psalm 150 from *A Book of Psalms: Selected and Adapted from the Hebrew* by Stephen Mitchell.

"Scraping the Blackened Bottom." The Anne Bradstreet (ca. 1612–72) lines incorporated into this poem are from her poem "To My Dear and Loving Husband."

The Ogishi named in "Brushes" was the greatest Chinese writer, according to Henry P. Bowie. His book *On the Laws of Japanese Painting* was the source for much of this poem, as well as for the poem "Japanese Wall Hanging."